ROWLEY LEIGH

Photography by SIMON WHEELER

THE MASTER CHEFS

TED SMART

ROWLEY LEIGH was born in Manchester in 1950. He lived in various parts of the UK as a child, including five years in Northern Ireland. A variety of educational establishments attempted to teach him, and after being rejected by almost every university in Britain he read English at Cambridge University. Leaving without a degree, he tried country life and farming for a few years before coming to London in 1976.

Falling into cooking because he needed a job in a hurry he spent eighteen months at Joe Allen's in Covent Garden before going to work for Roux restaurants in 1979. He was a cook at Le Gavroche, a pâtissier, a meat buyer and finally head chef at Le Poulbot for three years.

Rowley Leigh opened Kensington Place in London's Notting Hill with Nick Smallwood and Simon Slater in 1987 and is still there. In 1995 he became a columnist on *The Guardian*. He is married and has two children.

CONTENTS

Forget not the salt.

RECIPE FOR SPICE CAKE IN
A TRUE GENTLEWOMAN'S DELIGHT (1653)
ELIZABETH DE GREY,
COUNTESS OF KENT

INTRODUCTION

There is an excitement about wild food that is absent from its cultivated cousins. It's exciting partly because it is very seasonal, and we have a feeling of good fortune when we find it in season. It's exciting sometimes because it is, with the exception of game, free. It's exciting like any treasure hunt: whose pulse can fail to quicken at the sight of two or three morels poking through the grass in the corner of some field? In the case of game, it becomes a sport, and whether you choose to participate or not, that, too, is clearly very exciting.

The excitement of wild food doesn't stop at the finding of it. There is an intensity of flavour that is often missing in the cultivated or farmed equivalent.

Happily, there are many wild foods that resist cultivation and can only be enjoyed in their wild state. Many of these are mentioned in this little book, and the existence of such delights as wild garlic, sea trout, and the many varieties of wild mushrooms is a cause for constant celebration.

Rowley Leigh

WILD GARLIC SOUP

3 POTATOES, SLICED

1 LITRE/1¾ PINTS CHICKEN STOCK,
  OR WATER

1 LEMON

SALT AND PEPPER

25 G/1 OZ BUTTER

2 ONIONS, SLICED

A COLANDER FULL OF WASHED
  WILD GARLIC

GRATED NUTMEG

SOUR CREAM OR CRÈME FRAÎCHE

CROÛTONS

25 G/1 OZ BUTTER

3 SLICES OF DAY-OLD COUNTRY-
  STYLE BREAD, TORN INTO
  ROUGH CUBES

SERVES 4

Place the potatoes in a saucepan with the stock or water, a strip of lemon zest and plenty of salt and pepper. Simmer for 10–15 minutes.

Meanwhile, melt the butter in another saucepan and cook the onions over a low heat until soft. Turn up the heat, add the wild garlic, a little lemon juice, salt, pepper and nutmeg and cook until the garlic has wilted considerably. Add to the potatoes and stock and simmer together for 5 minutes, then purée in a liquidizer.

To make the croûtons, melt the butter in a frying pan and fry the bread until it is crisp and golden.

Serve the soup with a swirl of sour cream or crème fraîche and the buttery croûtons.

OMELETTE WITH MOUSSERONS

3 EGGS

50 G/2 OZ BUTTER

A HANDFUL OF MOUSSERON
   MUSHROOMS, CLEANED
   (PAGE 30)

SALT AND PEPPER

LEMON JUICE

SERVES 1

Break the eggs into a bowl and beat them lightly until they are thoroughly mixed.

Heat half the butter in a saucepan until it is foaming; fry the mushrooms very quickly and season with a little salt, pepper and lemon juice.

Place an omelette pan over a fairly high heat and add the remaining butter; when it is foaming, pour in the eggs, add the mushrooms and season well. Do nothing for 10 seconds, but wait for the eggs to bubble up in the middle of the pan. Stir quickly and lightly with the back of a fork or a wooden spoon, then move the omelette off the centre of the pan towards the edge of the pan furthest away from you. Speed is of the essence; the omelette should remain creamy in the centre and should take no more than 45 seconds to cook. Give the pan a little knock to nudge the omelette against the edge. Tip the omelette on to a warmed plate and serve at once, either on its own or with some fried potatoes.

CEPS WITH PARSLEY AND GARLIC

450 G/1 LB CEPS, CLEANED
   (PAGE 30)
3–4 TABLESPOONS OLIVE OIL
6 GARLIC CLOVES, FINELY CHOPPED
6 SPRIGS OF PARSLEY, FINELY
   CHOPPED
SALT AND PEPPER

SERVES 4

Slice the ceps quite thinly and sauté in olive oil in a very hot frying pan for 3–4 minutes. Using a slotted spoon, remove the ceps from the pan and keep warm.

Add a little more oil to the pan if necessary, then reduce the heat and add the garlic; cook for about 5 minutes, then return the ceps to the pan, add the parsley and season well. Serve immediately, either on their own or with a good steak.

STEAMED TURBOT
with horns of plenty

A HANDFUL OF HORN OF PLENTY
   MUSHROOMS, CLEANED
   (PAGE 30)
2 TABLESPOONS EXTRA VIRGIN
   OLIVE OIL
1 SMALL TURBOT, ABOUT
   900 G/2 LB, CLEANED, SKINNED
   AND FILLETED
1–2 GARLIC CLOVES, FINELY
   CHOPPED
1 TABLESPOON SNIPPED FRESH
   CHIVES

BEURRE BLANC

2 TABLESPOONS DRY WHITE WINE
1 TABLESPOON WHITE WINE
   VINEGAR
1 SHALLOT, FINELY CHOPPED
125 G/4 OZ COLD UNSALTED
   BUTTER, CUBED

SERVES 2

To make the butter sauce, put the wine, vinegar and chopped shallot in a small, heavy saucepan and boil until the liquid is reduced almost to nothing. Add the butter a little at a time, whisking vigorously, until it forms a creamy sauce – this should take no more than 2–3 minutes. Still whisking vigorously, increase the heat and bring the sauce to just below boiling point, then season to taste and remove from the heat. Keep warm by sitting the pan in a larger pan filled with very hot water.

Sauté the mushrooms in olive oil for about 2 minutes or until tender. Keep warm.

Steam the turbot fillets for 7–8 minutes or until cooked.

Serve at once, on warmed plates; top with the sauce, the mushrooms and a sprinkling of garlic and chives.

SEA TROUT FILLET
with a horseradish crust

2 KG/4½ LB SEA TROUT, CLEANED,
    SKINNED AND FILLETED, BONES
    RESERVED
50 G/2 OZ BUTTER
2 SHALLOTS, SLICED
1 GLASS OF DRY WHITE WINE
6 BLACK PEPPERCORNS
A SPRIG OF THYME
100 ML/3½ FL OZ DOUBLE CREAM
SALT AND PEPPER
LEMON
100 G/3½ OZ HORSERADISH,
    PEELED
100 G/3½ OZ DRIED BREADCRUMBS
4 TABLESPOONS FLOUR
1 EGG, BEATEN

SERVES 6

Rub your fingers over the fish to make sure no small bones remain; if you feel any, pull them out with a pair of tweezers.

Heat half the butter in a saucepan over a low heat and cook the shallots until soft but not browned. Add the chopped backbone of the trout, turn to seal in the butter, then add the wine, peppercorns and thyme and cook very gently for 10 minutes.

Add the cream and cook for another 10 minutes. Season well with salt, pepper and a squeeze of lemon juice. Strain through a fine sieve and boil to reduce slightly if the sauce is too thin. Keep warm.

Grate the horseradish very finely (this might make you cry) and mix with the breadcrumbs and a little salt and pepper. Dredge the trout fillets in a little flour and shake off any excess. Dip one side of each fillet in a little beaten egg and then into the breadcrumb and horseradish mixture.

Heat the remaining butter in a frying pan and fry the fillets, crumb side first, for about 4 minutes on each side. They should be very moist and remain slightly pink in the middle.

Serve the trout fillets on a bed of spinach, surrounded by the creamy sauce.

WILD SALMON WITH SORREL

EXTRA VIRGIN OLIVE OIL

4 THICK SALMON STEAKS, SKIN ON

1 LARGE BUNCH OF SORREL
  LEAVES, WASHED

1 LEMON

SEA SALT

COARSELY GROUND BLACK PEPPER

SERVES 4

Heat a heavy frying pan with a little oil, add the salmon steaks, skin side down, and cook very slowly for 10 minutes, or until the salmon is cooked half way through.

Pour out any excess oil and add the washed sorrel leaves. Turn the salmon steaks and squeeze in the juice of the lemon. Enrobe each steak with the wilted sorrel leaves, then remove from the pan while they are still very pink on the side away from the skin.

Serve at once, on warmed plates; pour the pan juices over the steaks, drizzle on a little extra virgin olive oil and scatter with sea salt and coarsely ground pepper.

CHICKEN WITH MORELS

100 G/3½ OZ FRESH MORELS
1 CHICKEN, CUT INTO 8 PIECES
SALT AND PEPPER
50 G/2 OZ BUTTER
1 GLASS OF DRY WHITE WINE
4 SHALLOTS, VERY FINELY CHOPPED
200 ML/7 FL OZ DOUBLE CREAM

SERVES 4

Wash the morels well, drain on a clean tea towel and then cut in half or into strips.

Season the chicken pieces and brown in the butter in a heavy saucepan over a low heat, skin side down. Turn and continue to cook very gently. When nearly cooked, pour out any excess fat and add the wine, scraping up the juices, and then boil until the wine has almost completely evaporated.

Add a little more butter and the shallots, and cook until they are soft, but without colour.

Add the morels and cook gently for 2–3 minutes.

Add the cream, turn the chicken in the sauce and bring to the boil. Simmer gently until the sauce is well reduced. Serve with rice pilaff cooked in chicken stock.

WILD RABBIT
with nettles, onions and cider

85 G/3 OZ BUTTER
6 ONIONS, THINLY SLICED
1 WILD RABBIT, JOINTED
SALT AND PEPPER
4 TABLESPOONS FLOUR
2 TABLESPOONS OLIVE OIL
500 ML/16 FL OZ CIDER
2 SPRIGS OF THYME
1 BAY LEAF
A LARGE HANDFUL OF NETTLES,
    WASHED, LEAVES PICKED OFF
1 TEASPOON ENGLISH MUSTARD

SERVES 4

Melt 25 g/1 oz of the butter in a casserole over a low heat and cook the onions until soft.

Season the rabbit pieces, dredge in a little flour and shake off any excess. Heat the oil and another 25 g/1 oz butter in a frying pan; add the rabbit pieces and brown all over.

Add the rabbit to the casserole with the onions. Pour out the fat from the frying pan and add some of the cider; stir over a fairly high heat to deglaze, then add to the rabbit together with the remaining cider. Add the thyme and bay leaf, bring to a gentle boil and simmer very gently for 1¼ hours.

Add the washed nettle leaves and simmer for another 15 minutes. The rabbit should now be very tender. Transfer the rabbit pieces to warmed plates. Add the mustard and the remaining butter to the sauce, taste and adjust the seasoning and pour over the rabbit.

WILD DUCK WITH BLACKBERRIES

1 WILD DUCK

2 SHALLOTS, ROUGHLY CHOPPED

1 CARROT, ROUGHLY CHOPPED

1 STICK OF CELERY, ROUGHLY
   CHOPPED

A SPRIG OF THYME

25 G/1 OZ BUTTER

2 TEASPOONS SUGAR

225 G/8 OZ BLACKBERRIES

1 TEASPOON RED WINE VINEGAR

1 GLASS OF RED WINE

SALT AND PEPPER

SERVES 2

Preheat the oven to 230°C/
450°F/Gas Mark 8.

Put the duck in a small,
flameproof roasting pan and roast
for 10 minutes. Add the vegetables
and thyme to the roasting pan and
cook for a further 10 minutes.

Remove the duck from the pan
and leave to rest in a warm place
for 10 minutes.

Add the butter and sugar to the
vegetables in the roasting pan and
brown over a fairly high heat.

Add half the blackberries and
continue cooking over a high heat
until their liquid has evaporated.
Add the vinegar and cook until it
has reduced away. Add the wine.

Remove the legs from the
duck, add to the sauce and simmer
gently for 15 minutes.

Carve the duck breast and serve
on warmed plates with a few
blackberries. Arrange the duck legs
on the plates, strain over the sauce
and serve at once.

WILD STRAWBERRY PUDDING

250 ML/8 FL OZ MILK
1 VANILLA POD, SPLIT IN HALF
3 GELATINE LEAVES
4 EGG YOLKS
100 G/3½ OZ CASTER SUGAR
225–250 G/8–9 OZ WILD
    STRAWBERRIES
250 ML/8 FL OZ DOUBLE OR
    WHIPPING CREAM

SERVES 4

Bring the milk to the boil with the vanilla pod, then leave to infuse for 20 minutes. Soak the gelatine leaves in some tepid water.

Whisk the egg yolks and sugar together until thick and pale, pour over the hot milk and return to the heat. Cook slowly, stirring constantly with a wooden spoon until the mixture begins to thicken. Remove from the heat, add the drained gelatine, whisk well and leave to cool.

Add the wild strawberries to the custard. Whip the cream to a soft ribbon consistency and fold into the custard. Pour into one large mould or four small moulds. Place in the refrigerator and leave until set.

If you have some more strawberries and some are a little soft, purée them in a liquidizer with a little caster sugar to make a coulis to serve with the pudding.

THE BASICS

GLOSSARY

Most of these foods are available, free, in the wild, at certain times of year. Mushrooms will usually be earlier in southern England and if weather conditions are favourable. Game is protected by season, and you will need a licence and to pay for the privilege of shooting or fishing it.

BLACKBERRIES
Wild blackberries are smaller and tastier than cultivated varieties. Found in hedgerows throughout the UK. August and September.

CEPS
(Boletus edulis) Also known as the penny bun, which describes the caps of these excellent, firm-textured mushrooms. Known as *cèpes* in French, *porcini* in Italian. Found in woodland, usually after rain. July–October.

DUCK
Wild duck, sometimes available from butchers with a game dealer's licence, includes mallard, widgeon and teal. The season is September and October.

GARLIC (WILD)
Found in woodland, often near bluebells. April–June.

HORNS OF PLENTY
(Craterellus cornucopioides) The tubular shape and dark brown or black colour give rise to the French name, *trompette de la mort* (trumpet of death). Despite this name, they are delicious. Found in woodland. July–October.

HORSERADISH
A tall plant with big, shabby leaves, horseradish is sometimes found in the wild, an escapee from gardens. Only the root is used, peeled and grated.

MORELS

(*Morchella esculenta*) The honeycombed cap is pale yellow-brown, darkening with age. Grows in grassland, near or in the shadow of beech trees. April–June.

MOUSSERONS

(*Marasmius oreades*) Small, pale tan coloured, surprisingly tasty mushroom, taking its common name, Fairy Ring Champignon, from its habit of growing in circles, in pastureland and on lawns. April–June.

NETTLES

Easy enough to find, but make sure they are away from roads or other sources of pollution. Use rubber gloves to pick the tender young leaves in spring. April–June.

RABBIT

Wild rabbit is tastier but tougher than the domesticated, or farmed, version. All year round, but best in summer.

SALMON (WILD)

The fishing season for wild salmon is March–September. The flavour is at its best early in the season.

SEA TROUT

The same season as wild salmon. Brown trout is the same species.

SORREL

Easily cultivable, but often grows prolifically in the wild. April–June.

STRAWBERRIES

Tiny, pretty and very low-fruiting woodland plant. April–June.

NOTES ON WILD MUSHROOMS

Procure a well-respected and well-illustrated text book on mushrooms and learn to identify the dangerous ones. Never cook a mushroom unless you are absolutely sure what it is you are cooking.

Go mushroom hunting early in the morning, to beat other foragers off the mark, and to get the mushrooms at their best. Collect them in a flat basket, and always carry a sharp knife, so that you may cut them cleanly at the stem. Specialist mushroom knives have a little brush at the other end to get rid of any loose spores, or twigs and grass.

When preparing mushrooms, never leave them to soak in water. When possible, just wipe with a damp cloth or brush or scrape away any dirt. Cut away any spongy or rotten parts. Larger mushrooms such as ceps need to have their stems peeled. If you do have to wash mushrooms, drop them gently into a bowl of cold salted water and immediately lift them out again. This will get rid of the dirt and free them of any strands of vegetation. Gently dry them in a colander. Morels, with their honeycombed caps, need to be well washed.

When cooking wild mushrooms, those with a high water content will first need to be 'blanched'. Heat a little olive oil in a frying pan until very hot, throw in the mushrooms, leave them for 1 minute, then toss them in the pan and drain in a colander over a bowl to collect the liquid. This is a kind of mushroom stock, and is very good in soups, sauces and risottos. Some mushrooms, such as morels and the smaller ceps, are best cooked from raw, and their juices reduced with the mushrooms themselves.